In the boat I don't yet have

In the boat I don't yet have

Collected Poems

Aidan McEoin

ISBN 0-9541771-0-X

A catalogue record for this book is available from the British Library

Cover photograph: © Axel Nehen

Printed in Scotland
by Govan Litho Printing and Design Co-operative
First printing 500. Second printing 500.

Published by Singing Sands

Ground Left
33 Nithsdale Road
Strathbungo
Glasgow
G41 2AL

Contact: Andrew Binnie
E-mail: acbinnie@yahoo.com

Singing Sands
Glasgow Sydney Isle of Eigg

Contents

Beans on Toast

Beans on toast
Not gourmet to most
But I for one
Am proud to boast
I've had them for
Breakfast dinner and tea
Now you tell me
Where you get all three
All for just 21p
Three meals in one
With plenty of gas
If you'll pardon the pun
I open the can
Then into the pot
Then onto the plate
And I begin to ate
With pepper and salt
And washed down
With a malt
Sure it's like the Ritz
Instead of the pits
The temptations upon me
To eat the lot
But 'tis only the morn
And it's all I got
So I cover the pot
And save the rest
For the evenin' slot.

Cog

How often
must I feel despair
only to respite itself once again
into the lurking shadows of my mind?
My life, it seems,
is constantly at the eleventh hour:
I surface,
just when it seems I'm about
to drown.
I've immersed myself in the search
of truth
and society has answered me bluntly,
as bluntly
as an unsharpened knife
being used to take my heart
from within.
Well fuck yourself!
See,
look,
my heart is beating.
You can starve and penetrate me,
You can violate my mind
with your social ethics;
you can instruct me
through your medium of
institutionalisation
on how I should be;
you can share nothing of your system
with me

You make me feel inhuman.
Look,
look you fucker,
you're the one in the cage,
you've drowned.
You throw lame strokes at me
'cause I'm swimming overhead you.
You.
You
can't even see my face.

Without a Cigarette

I am hungry and fagless
in this stony city:
I have walked the streets
Trying my best to look
Destitute.
I can't.

I marvel at the
Singular architecture
That encloses its inhabitants
As they move about their daily
Chores.
Positive laughter rings in my
Ears.
Wanton folly by the young
Taken for what it is by the old.
Alive – they are all so
Alive.

It's times like these I really
Need a cigarette.
Smoke to their health –
if I had one I would.
Sit on this bench
Or on any bench and puff quite
Contentedly:
But I haven't so I can't.
I know one would cure this
Hunger pang.
But I also know if I have
One,
I must have twenty.
I'm a bit greedy like that.

The Dripping Tap

The tap drips – pools of wasted water,
Delft piled high
Mildewing its contents.
The ironing board – idle in the corner,
The table bare
There's nothing to share.
But for the dripping tap
Bringing me along with its
Inane unwanted madness.
Inner anger with myself, with the world,
With the dripping tap.

Jesus, what a total desperate situation
Fucking reduced to the company

Of a dripping tap.
A worrying thought, I listen
Continually, consistently
And revel in the fact
That I can't stop it.
I can't control it.
I can only run from it.
But it's there again the next day,
The next week,
The next month.
The dripping tap – into pools of
Wasted water.

I take the chance and
Turn the tap – I turn the tap
The drip is a flow.
I turn the tap
The flow is a gush.
I turn the tap
The gush is a spray.
I place my finger under the tap
The spray spreads.
I turn the tap
The spray is a gush.
I turn the tap
The gush is a flow.
I turn the tap
The flow is a drip.
I turn the tap
It remains a drip.
But for the dripping tap
Silence – deadly silence.

Giro Day

O' Giro day, O' Giro day
I get my pay
And drink for the day.
'Tis mean of me
Some might say:
To hell with the begrudgers
'Tis Giro day.

I cash it in
And go without,
I head for town
for a drinkin' bout,
I meet my friends
The few that are left,
We sit in the bars
And have a few jars.

We chat about life
And all its strife
And thank the Lord we haven't a wife.
O' Giro day, O' Giro day,
I get my pay
and drink for the day.

I go to Sandy's for a few Bell's
Washed down with pints of black nectar –
Sure there's nothin' next to her –
Then down to the square
And into the Tron,

'Tis a very rare night you won't hear a song
A couple in there
And beginning to feel square;
Then up to the Oak
To have the last spoke.

Palpitations set in
As my thoughts are on sin
I foam at the mouth
but only bubbles come out.

I head for home backwards
Without even a forward glace
Asking everyone I meet,
"Would ye like to dance?"
"Shag off!", they say
As they go on their way.
"You're right", says I
With a woeful sigh.

I wake the next day
With my head gone astray,
And wait
For the next
Giro day.

I hope

I hope, that there's hope
For us, that hope
That there's hope
I hope.

Through the End of a Glass

The inner confusion of one's mind,
conflicting with outer emotions
leaves one drained and remorseful –
escapism through the end of a glass.
Uninhibited honesty
while it lasts.
I cannot begin to find a
different solution.
The individuality of oneself
is made up of so many individualities.
Who is normal?
Who is sane?
Life can give so much pain.
You drain every happiness
Through the end of a glass
Only to refill it
And welcome blissed abyss.

One Dram Too Many

The vibrancy
When the bottle's uncorked
The euphoria
When the cork is thrown into the fire
The knowledge, that
Springs to mind, a third of the way down
The omniscience
When halfway down
The aggressiveness
Towards the bottom
One last attempt, the bottles empty
So is the room.

Life's Smell

Street faces telling me it's important
Office faces telling me more so
News readers dead pan
Clergy sanctimonious thumping
Lawyers in disguise
Friends faces distorted
Hearts soured and embittered
Banal conversations in vogue
Everybody loves a rogue
From a distance
Shit upon others
As you perceive they shit upon you

Take, take, take,
Don't give
Shouldn't give
Why do you give?
It's smelly
Pardon me?
No
What's smelly?
Ever take a deep smell here?
No way
Why?
Because it smells of shit
But that's life.

People

people on a make
people on a take
people on a break
people on the fiddle
people on a diddle
people on people
people on people
they all fall down.

It

It is as it is
One can never change it
One can never be it
Yet we strive for it

We live for it
We aspire to it
We never accept it
But it will always be
It.

Access 1

Mature struggle
Beneath their cloaks of rule
Immense confusion – just like school
Each trying to hide the fool
Behind what has been the rule
No mere person am I
No mere person are you
Yet we're marked as equal
In your eyes
As scholastic tools
We go to the pub at night
Unleash our unspoken shite
In the hope that we might
Gain access – for foresight
Our inner thoughts spoken aloud
Safe in the knowledge
We've got a sympathetic crowd
Access to a higher degree
Notions of betterment
It seems to me
It's a rational thing to expand
Our expansion is for us
To understand

And not for you to disregard
Out of hand
Be it so
We were all that grand

Shadows

By candlelit shadows
Throwing shapes
Without form at first,
The flickering unity
Seems to escape
Not knowing
Others
Are flickering for the same place
The same shape.

Harris (On the Isle of Rum)

Your legacy of ruined settlements
Seem restless, disturbed
By neglect of successive
Overlords that foolishly
Thought money could buy
What people had freely.
Unlike you, they bought
What they could never own,
The natural affinity that
Binds the land and the people.

Limitless time has withstood
The follies of egocentrics
From fantasy to
Ardent perusal of the academic
Laws of nature.
Production line regeneration
Serves only to remind
What was natural
In an unnatural
Clinical way.
Void of the souls
That lived in reality with
Nature,
That limitless and priceless
Affinity that binds
The land and the people
Naturally

Tribute to Sorley MacLean

You've left your shore behind
Again and again we'll walk along it.
Aspiring to grasp what you saw so clearly
In moments of poetic clarity.
Infused with the spirit of the Gael,
The moon was full on the night you departed
Justly so.
Leaving us a little light through the
Sorrowful knowledge that you'll not walk
Among us in this world again

Not so, that we can see you, but remember.
To those that look, we can read you through
Your pen,
And think, again and again
Upon your Celtic shore, the image that maybe
You've walked this way before.
Hurry your passage to the court of
Tir-Na-nOg where
Your equals await,
Beannach de libh.

A Girl with Copper Tinted Hair

Animated radiance of
Copper tinted hair
Curt features
So aware
Contrasting red coat
Awareness
So rare
That I in my drunken glance
Can only stare
Words fail me
To express what I fear
Who are you close to
And are they here?
Yes
You of the copper tinted hair
In tune with your

Autumnal surroundings
I am here
Alas, you are there.

Tidal Lovers

I'm sitting on Weymouth harbour,
right in front of me is the sea.
The harbour lights dance boldly
upon its reflecting image.
Two lovers have stopped in front of me –
she is wearing a cocktail dress,
he's taking his boots off.
How beautifully romantic.
They walk hand in hand
towards the sea and obscurity
professing their lust
for one another.

I've just spotted a solitary figure.
She looks as dejected
as I sometimes feel.
She seems to have lost
the momentary feeling of escapism.
I wish you luck.

The two lovers
have materialised in front of me again,
professing their undying friendship,
etching their names together

in a sand-made heart,
happy in the knowledge
that the early morning tide
will have carried away
all traces of the pact made
the night before.

Who Else

Who else but you
Saw through the tapestry
My friend?
Who else but you
Saw through the barriers
I'd raised?
Who else but you could reverse it
And lay it at my feet?
Who else am I to
Over indulge
Expressing
I don't need?
Who else but you sees through
The tapestry?

Friendship

Never before has contentment
Set in so readily;
Acceptance and to be accepted

in surroundings that only a
Short time ago were unknown
To me,
Yet surroundings that are familiar to my heart;
Surface deep but warm,
Ready to expand
On both levels
Given the chance.
Friendship:
A rarity and beauty
Shared
Only by those
Who seek it.

Memory of a Love

My thoughts are of you
My blonde haired beauty
With eyes of blue;
And I'd been cautioned
That I'd one day rue
The day I met you
And was compelled to woo.

I think of times past
With sorrow in my heart,
For even then my love
I knew it wouldn't last.
Too much had happened
in our individual pasts
To allow our bonding in that surrounding.

I remember with fondness
The aspirations we shared.
The world could have stopped,
We wouldn't have cared.
My life was yours
And yours was mine
But destiny had it so
They would never entwine.

There's a part of me
Will always be yours.
I wonder how you are,
For thoughts of you are seldom far
From my memory of a love
That has been and gone.
May you find another
And, with my love, carry on.

Leaving

I must leave now,
I must be on my way.
You've gotten close enough,
I really cannot stay.
I wounded you
Through my selfish inadequate way
It hurts me more than you think it may,
I'm not without feeling –
That to me you did teach
I just couldn't grasp it,

It was out of my reach.
I can't accept what you give freely:
I know it will cost me dearly.
As I move away
And block you out
You must know it was I did doubt.
I can't be at one
For what's done is done.
With deepest regards
I'll see you anon.

I Thought I'd Forgotten

It was you that I saw in my dream
One day long ago.
I'd thought I'd forgotten,
For a time I did.
You've materialised in form,
Rumbling through the rubble
Of barriers that have fallen
Powerless to your truth.
I respond with honesty
As I did in my dream,
Welcoming you in my reality
With friendship, trust and respect –
With a oneness so rare.
I'd thought I'd forgotten,
For a time I did
You've revived an emotion
Within me

That has so much to give,
To share, to hold,
To lean upon.
I'm there and here now
One day long ago.
I'd though I'd forgotten,
For a time I did.

My confusion is my reality:
Deep down inside
A flame flickers,
Responding to the fire of
Conviction
That burns within you.
Your strength of resolve
A beacon
To the weakness of those and I
Who would shut out
Human compassion towards
Others that are vulnerable
For nothing other than a
Possession
That could never truly be possessed if
Stained or tainted with a narrow mind,
A selfish ego, and unjust love.
An acceptance with a humility
Of your hurtful honesty –
An inspirational testimony
To those and I
Who are fortunate to share.
My strengths are within –
Safe, unworthy

Until now.
I offer them to you
Without condition, with all I am
Capable of.
The flickering flame
Responds, with love.

First Snow on the Hills

Patches of snow salt the hills
In contrast with the brown heather,
That's usurped by the first whiteness
That falls where it will, unchallenged
Upon the tops of the wilderness
Where it remains, untouched
Until it dissolves itself
As silently, as it came.

Winter's Come

Sleet rain, not yet snow
It's not far away
Cold frost mornings
Breath thaws
Mitten covered paws
Stem the burning freeze
Harsh southwesterly breeze
Whips the loch
Winter's come.

Winter Night

Wet black night
Howling wind echo's
Through the glens
The bark of the rutting stag
Looking for the hind
It can't find
Mid the lashing rain.

Swans in Snow at Arthur's Seat

White snow falling softly
Resting at the end of
Arthur's seat
White swans poised
In graceful acceptance of the
Elements
Unmoving in the brilliant whiteness
Only akin to themselves
Unflustered proud they stay
Unmoved
Only they identify with the
Virginal surroundings
That propels humanity into chaos
Such tiny flakes
In such vast multitudes
The swan accepts
With its tranquil wonderment
With its virginal ease and beauty.

Duvet of Nature

Such purity I acknowledge in a
Moment passing:
I gaze in wonderment
As the white duvet
Of nature
Encompasses its distant
Brethren.
It silently visits their
Crags and peaks.
Their branches,
Their limbs,
Cleansing them unhurriedly,
Softly
Resting and sleeping itself
Into their very core.
The murkiness of the winter rain
Enveloped within their flakes,
The duvet of nature
Cleansing its mother
With the ultimate caress of
Softness.

My walk on Binn Mountain

The tranquillity that
Billows through my very
Skin,
My thoughts are left
Unclouded.
I stand in the face
Of the December sea gale
As it engulfs my entire
Being.
I struggle to walk
The well-worn path,
Determined to reach my
Goal –
I've lost it for now
In my billowing surrounds.
The wind pierces my
Very thoughts;
Such wonderful respite
From the winters rage
I find in this sparse ravine.
My emotions change accordingly
With the inner glow
I feel;
To identify with these
Elements,
Such a humble ism.
Such a loss for me
It is to reach
Its very foundation.

The Lammerlaws

I close my eyes and hear
The gently chants of the Lammerlaws.
I feel them move around me,
The hooded ghosts of the
Silent lammerlaws;
The ruins of a once flourishing
If silent community,
Buried beneath vegetation
Sealing its fate,
Its secrets, its knowledge
Of what had been
And gone.
Cindered and scorched into
Oblivion.
The gentle lap lapping of the
Sea
Whispering to the monastic
Ghosts of the Lammerlaws,
"Your secret is safe with me".
"How did it happen?", I ask it
"Ask the rock your sitting on", it replies
I'll not tell him the rock
Stonily answers us both
"Its very peaceful here", I say,
"Yes", they reply
"Yes", I say.

The Sea Shanty

His memories spiral
Around and upward.
Like the smoke from the pipe
He holds with his one good hand.
He sits on the pier, still.
His eyes gaze outward
Across the expanse that
Hold his memories
Along with the sea shanty
He hums quietly,
He heard it somewhere,
But not here.

Unity

She's not happy beached
She lists to the left,
gaping,
speechless in her acceptance.
Powerless without me,
as I am without her.
At sea
we need each other
and the oars need us,
both.
We're a unit.
But I must make the first move,

and decide what's best,
in consultation
with the tide,
that ebbs and flows
in time, that is without
time
as ancient as the roof above it,
my only overhead.
The moon,
waxing lyrical
to my aspirations
and the boat
I don't yet have.

Ides of March

I could take three or four
my love and I, two more.
We could leave the shore,
my love at the bow
and I at the oar;
between us,
would sit,
our two more.
Padded, just in case
though chaste,
the two would have no fear
of the deep, deep
depth, that holds
my love and my
deepest unspoken fear.

The Merciless Sea

The mighty swells
of winter gales,
lashed with hail and rain.
Little point of my testing my mettle
against such force,
hands at the tiller
just holding on, nothing more.
The sea swallowing me
then spitting me out;
a repetitive game
she likes to play.
Heave Ho Ho Ho
she tosses me to an fro.
Then, with a sideward,
nonchalant push,
I land on her shore,
while she crashes in rage against the rocks
around me.
I hasten from her wrath
And thank her for her small mercy.
She swells and whips along,
merciless.
Leaving me in little doubt
mercy was not her intent
Nor, ever will be.

In the Boat I Don't Yet Have

In the boat I don't yet have
I would be sustainable.
Though,
the boat and I should be
seaworthy and able.
The pots, properly baited
would, in a few days
suffice my hunger.
Sated.
And the line hooked around my finger,
patiently waiting,
beneath November's ice blue sky,
for the tug
and success.

The Boat

Planked, planed
and varnished.
Caulked, secure
and proud.
With the mystical shroud
of the ancient mariners
that sat in her
before I,
and left her in a state
of readiness;
for my maiden voyage.

Tentative strokes
with the seasoned oars,
I venture out.
She acknowledges my trepidation,
responding to my
erratic course
and with years of experience,
gently coaxes me
into her trust.

Confessional

I stand at the shore
and think again
on what I
don't yet have
but other do rue.
The hesitant spirit
if only I had the strength
of conviction, that I may
serve upon myself
the indulgence gained
by confessing the truth
to myself, rather than to another
who gives me penance
opposed to freedom,
the freedom the boat would give to me
without condition.
Allow me to escape for a while
alone, but would, in time

bring me ashore, once more
to realise my penance.
Absolution lasts a short time only,
And life, goes on.

The Dream

In my dream, she had
Eighteen masts and thirty six sails;
She was a feminist Neptune
A Boadicea of the sea,
Her presence warned
Long John and the likes to flee.
Captain Bligh was Her cabin boy
Fletcher Christian Her slave
Her phallic bow rode the mightiest wave.
Tidal storms she took in Her stride
Her gunwales inviting and open wide.
The sea was Her daughter.
Amid rolls and rolls of laughter,
She ploughed furrows that
are now straits.
And I,
Her captain, steered Her
To the largest and,
Most refined port.

Small Comfort

Angry white seahorses
Engulf the shoreline.
And my carcass,
Seeps in agony, yet
Silently waits to be
Sealed dry
From the incessant tide
Lapping at its hull
That is holed and bare
Against this onslaught.
I give it little comfort
With the patch of linoleum
I place over its most gaping hole
In minutes it becomes sodden,
And the boat, insulted.
I can do no more for it,
Yet if follows me home
To the warmth
And remains, within my heart.

Enchanted

We are more in fear of her
Than she is of us.
The sea.
At her best
Calm and serene
At her worst

A churning white tipped
Rabid bitch
That commands respect
But gives little in return,
She has no need to.
Unlike those who command
The boats that sail
Upon her and pander to
Her mood swings,
Highs and lows.
The elements in whatever guise
Serve only to compliment her
Whilst we, mere mortals,
Fall deeper and deeper
Under her spell.

Am Maighdain-Mhara

Chan eil fhios agam
Cuin a bhios me ullamh
Gu faigh me bata mo fhein
Ach nuair a thig an latha sin
Bidh mi saor.
Gu seachranaich am muir
Rannsachadh airson an
Maighdean-mhara sin a'fuireach
Fo an uisce liathghorm
Tha i a'cumail
De an seoladair
Bidh me a'faighneachd dhi

De th'agam re dheanamh
Gun can i rium
Rinn thu sin cheana agus
Bheir i mi leatha
Fo an uisce liathghorm.

A Suidhe ann am Bata

Bidoh i beag
Ach triese agus
Chen eil i
Draghail
Chan eil i crosda
Anns a'madinn
Nuair a tha e fuar.
Bidh mi a suidhe
Le mo fhein air an
Abhainn, anns a'bhata
Bidh e samhach agus
Siochail
Bidh mi a'rannschadh air
An saoghal mun cuairt orm
Smaointeachadh
Nach e tha alainn.